# Best Easy Day Hikes
# Hawaii: Maui

## Help Us Keep This Guide Up to Date

Every effort has been made by the author and editors to make this guide as accurate and useful as possible. However, many things can change after a guide is published—trails are rerouted, regulations change, facilities come under new management, etc.

We would appreciate hearing from you concerning your experiences with this guide and how you feel it could be improved and kept up to date. While we may not be able to respond to all comments and suggestions, we'll take them to heart and we'll also make certain to share them with the author. Please send your comments and suggestions to the following address:

Globe Pequot Press
Reader Response/Editorial Department
P.O. Box 480
Guilford, CT 06437

Or you may e-mail us at:

editorial@GlobePequot.com

Thanks for your input, and happy trails!

Best Easy Day Hikes Series

# Best Easy Day Hikes
# Hawaii: Maui

**Suzanne Swedo**

**FALCON**GUIDES

GUILFORD, CONNECTICUT
HELENA, MONTANA

AN IMPRINT OF GLOBE PEQUOT PRESS

*For William Goldsmith*

# FALCONGUIDES®

Project editor: Julie Marsh
Layout artist: Kevin Mak
Maps: Design Maps Inc. © Morris Book Publishing, LLC
TOPO! Explorer software and SuperQuad source maps courtesy of National Geographic Maps. For information about TOPO! Explorer, TOPO!, and Nat Geo Maps products, go to www.topo.com or www.natgeomaps.com.

Library of Congress Cataloging-in-Publication Data is available on file.
ISBN 978-0-7627-4348-3

Printed in the United States of America
10 9 8 7 6 5 4 3 2 1

# Contents

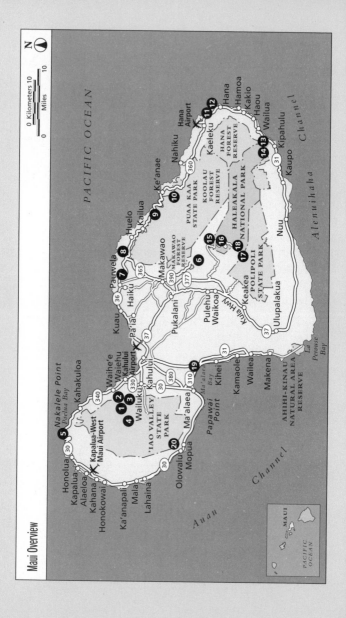

Maui Overview

# Acknowledgments

Thanks to Judy Edwards and Kiera Strom-Herman-Lyons at Haleakala National Park, Wade Holmes of the Hawai'i Nature Center, and Torrie L. Nohara at *Na Ala Hele* Hawai'i Trail & Access System, along with Melinda Goodwater and Singaman Lama, Rona Levein, Gordon Douglas, Pat Medley, Joellyn and Dave Acree, and Meryl Leventhal.

# Maui, the Valley Isle

Maui is the second biggest (next to Hawai'i) and the second most frequently visited (next to O'ahu) of the Hawaiian Islands. In recent years it has been growing fast, with resorts and condos creeping outward along formerly unspoiled coastlines on the leeward side of the island. But there is still enough wild country to explore—on mostly well-maintained trails—to keep hikers happy for months.

Named for Maui, the demigod who captured the sun and forced it to slow its progress across the sky, bringing longer, sunnier days to the island, it is also known as the Valley Isle because it's made up of two mountains joined by an isthmus. These two mountains are so different they might as well be separate islands, and a couple of times they have been. Sediments washed down the side of the older mountain, and lava flowed down from the newer one, to form the land connection—the "valley"—between them. At times of higher sea levels, when the climate warmed between glacial periods, the isthmus was inundated and the two mountains became separate islands. The deep sediments of the isthmus made it a rich agricultural area and sugarcane is still grown there, though plantations are disappearing as prices have fallen and development replaces agriculture.

The older volcano that formed West Maui is extinct now. It has been deeply grooved and weathered by wind and water and is clothed in dense vegetation. Pu'u Kukui on West Maui is second only to Mount Wai'ale'ale on Kaua'i in the amount of rainfall it receives (over 400 inches per year).

1

There are a number of river and ridgetop hikes on West Maui, including the beautiful 'Iao Valley, and you can get to most of them easily from Kahului, where the island's main population center and airport are. You can also find some of the island's cheapest accommodations in Wailuku, right next door. It's an interesting, slightly shabby old town—a little like Hilo on the Big Island—with a couple of hostels and inexpensive hotels.

The main tourist attraction on West Maui is the historical whaling port of Lahaina, on the leeward side. Lots of shops and restaurants line the pretty harbor. It is also a National Historic Landmark, with many of its original buildings restored and open to the public. It's fun to take a stroll down the main street but is a fairly expensive place to stay.

To the north, the resorts of Ka'anapali sprawl along beaches where snorkeling is great, but there isn't much for hikers except manicured paths through hotel grounds. More tourists gather in Kihea on the sunny southern side of the isthmus, where another string of condos, malls, and golf courses are crammed together for miles along the shore. Farther southwest there is still some undeveloped shoreline where you can find isolated bays and interesting trails. Partway between Lahaina and Kihea you'll find the tiny settlement of Olowalu, trailhead for a walk to a set of petroglyphs, mysterious designs chipped into the rock face by early Hawaiians. Their condition isn't perfect, but they *are* the real things.

Haleakala, the younger of the two volcanoes that make up Maui, emerged from the sea not much more than a million years ago, and has erupted within historic times so it is still considered active. At 10,023 feet it is twice as high as the highest of the West Maui mountains. Its northern coastline is surely one of the most beautiful in the world. The notorious Hana Highway winds past the trailheads for several hikes to waterfalls, nature preserves, and botanical gardens. Near its end is Hana, jumping-off point for hikes in the Kipahulu section of Haleakala National Park, home of the misnamed Seven Sacred Pools. The Hana Highway is such a long, slow drive that if you plan to hike from Kipahulu or explore any of the other trails nearby, you should stay somewhere near the eastern end of the island. Hana is charming but small, expensive, and often wet. There is a free campground at Kipahulu, but the real bargain in accommodations is at Wai'anapanapa State Park north of Hana. It has both camping and very inexpensive, fully equipped housekeeping cabins. For information call (808) 984-8109 (online reservations are not accepted). Some of Maui's most exciting treks begin at Wai'anapanapa, and it's a good place to watch for sea turtles, dolphins, and whales.

The most extensive system of trails is in Haleakala National Park. Some of these begin in the Kipahulu District on the coast, but there is a whole network of trails inside Haleakala Crater itself. Do not miss the chance to visit this volcano, even if you only have enough time to look over the edge. The scenery is wild and barren and indescribably beautiful, like nowhere else on earth. It is home to the endangered Hawaiian goose, the *nene,* and to the extremely rare silversword, which blooms with stalks of flowers up to 9 feet tall. Campgrounds and cabins inside the crater provide some of the few opportunities on Maui for multiday hikes or backpacking, but you can get a real feel for the place by hiking just a few hours, partway in and back out again, on one of two excellent trails. Take warm clothing, though. The rim of Haleakala is notorious for catching visitors unprepared for the chilly temperatures at 10,000 feet. It has been known to snow here in winter—even if it *is* the tropics.

## Maps

The shaded relief map of Maui published by the University of Hawai'i Press, available in bookstores and elsewhere, is the best for exploring the island as a whole. It gives you a bird's-eye view of the geography of the island including its mountains, waterfalls, beaches, and of course, its roads and highways.

The *Na Ala Hele* Trail and Access System, part of the Hawai'i Department of Land and Natural Resources, has online maps and information at www.hawaiitrails.org as well.

## Getting Around

There is no public transportation on Maui. If you are not a resident, you will need a rental car to get around. Keep in mind that though the island isn't big, roads are usually winding and travel is slow. Allow much more time than you think you need to get to a trailhead. For example, don't expect to drive from Kahului to Hana and still have time for a hike when you get there. The road to Haleakala Volcano, with its many hairpin turns, will take two to three hours from Kahului or Kihei, so plan accordingly. Remember to leave absolutely nothing in your car at trailheads.

# A Few Words of Caution

## Weather Patterns

Weather on Maui is usually lovely, with temperatures between 70 and 80 degrees year-round. There are essentially two seasons: Summer (May through October) is only slightly warmer than winter. The trade winds blowing from the northeast usually keep even the warmest days pleasant. Rainfall is lighter and of shorter duration in summer than in winter. Rainfall in winter is more frequent, heavier, and lasts longer, but is not likely to spoil most hikes unless it is brought by a Kona storm. These occur when for some reason or other the trade winds fail. Kona storms move in from the opposite direction than the trade winds, from the southwest instead of the northeast, and can pour down buckets for days on end. Always pack clothing to wear in layers, some synthetic rather than cotton for fast drying and to wick moisture away from your skin. A Windbreaker and rain gear are essential items to carry in your day pack. Make sure you have a brimmed hat and lots of sunscreen, too. The sun is directly overhead this close to the equator.

## Drinking Water

All free-flowing water on the islands must be treated before drinking. Leptospirosis is the most significant waterborne disease-causing organism in the Hawaiian Islands. It is spread primarily by rats, mice, and mongooses. It is a bacterium that can cause flulike symptoms including fever, diarrhea, nausea, muscle pain, chills, headache, and weakness, and if not treated with antibiotics, it can lead to very serious problems like heart or kidney failure.

Chemical treatment or boiling will take care of drinking water, but you can get leptospirosis by swimming in contaminated water as well as by drinking it. You are advised not to swim in fresh water if you have a cut or broken skin, and not to put your head underwater. That said, swimming and splashing in Maui's streams and pools is one of the most popular pastimes in the islands, and nobody appears to be overly concerned. But you should be aware that there is a risk.

## Stream Crossings

Speaking of water, it rains a lot on windward Maui and there are several hikes in this guide that involve stream crossings. Some are shallow enough to rock hop, though rocks are often rounded and slick and wading is safer. If it has been raining long and hard, streams may be too high and fast to ford safely.

Unexpected flash floods are especially dangerous and have killed lots of people. Many of Hawaii's streams flow down almost perpendicular cliffs, and floods may originate high up in the rainy mountains while you stroll unaware along the coast under sunny skies. If a stream appears muddy, or if you can hear rocks rolling along the streambed, turn around! Tropical vegetation often releases tannins into water, making it dark in color and hard to see through even under ordinary conditions, but swirling mud is serious.

## Waves, Currents, and Riptides

The sea currents around the islands have weird patterns. There are lovely quiet coves perfect for snorkeling and big regular waves for surfing, but in some places riptides can pull you off your feet and sweep you out to sea in an instant. Never turn your back on the ocean when exploring tide pools or walking along sea cliffs. A rogue wave can sneak up on you any time. Beaches where it is not safe to swim are almost always clearly marked with warning signs, and the signs mean business!

Hawai'i has experienced tsunamis (tidal waves) at rare intervals that killed many. You will probably notice yellow civil defense warning sirens on posts all over windward coastlines. If these begin to blow, get to higher ground immediately.

## Losing the Trail

Established trails on Maui are almost always easy to follow. If you become confused, turn around and go back to where you began, then start over. Don't compound a mistake by plunging farther and farther into the unknown. It is especially important to stay on designated trails in Hawai'i because dense forest vegetation can obscure boundaries of private property. Many routes skirt or cross private property where owners have granted hikers the right of way, but a *KAPU* (forbidden) sign means no trespassing.

Pig and goat hunting are time-honored pastimes in the islands. At present, hunting is permitted in certain areas on weekends and holidays, but schedules change. Trails in areas where hunting is allowed will usually have a sign saying so at the trailhead. If you stay on the trail and wear bright clothing, there is very little danger from hunters.

Sticking to the trail will also help you respect cultural traditions by steering you away from religious sites and cemeteries.

## Trailhead Vandalism

Vandalism is the most distressing, if not life-threatening, experience most hikers ever face. For the most part Hawaiians are friendly, helpful, and kind. Unfortunately there are always a few exceptions, and tourists are easy marks. Rental cars are usually obvious and tourists are apt to leave all sorts of belongings in them when they go off on a hike.

If you pull into a parking space at a remote trailhead and see broken glass on the ground, be warned. Leave absolutely nothing in your car, not even in the trunk. Generally, busy trailheads with people coming and going all day are safest. But don't spoil your visit by worrying about your car. The odds against being vandalized are in your favor, but you can greatly improve them by taking a few precautions.

## Zero Impact

We, as trail users, must be vigilant to make sure our passage leaves no lasting mark. Here are some basic guidelines for preserving trails in the region:

- Pack out all your own trash. You might also pack out garbage left by less-considerate hikers.
- Don't approach or feed any wild creatures—the crow eyeing your snack food is best able to survive if it remains self-reliant.
- Don't pick wildflowers or gather rocks, feathers, or other treasures along the trail. Removing these items will only take away from the next hiker's experience.
- Avoid damaging trailside soils and plants by remaining on the established route.
- Be courteous by not making loud noises while hiking.

- Many of these trails are multiuse, which means you'll share them with other hikers, trail runners, mountain bikers, and equestrians. Familiarize yourself with the proper trail etiquette, for example, yielding the trail when appropriate.
- Use outhouses at trailheads or along the trail.

# How to Use This Guide

To aid in quick decision making, each hike chapter begins with a hike summary. These short summaries give you a taste of the hiking adventure to follow. You'll learn what surprises the route has to offer. Next, you'll find the quick, nitty-gritty details of the hike: where the trailhead is located, hike length, approximate hiking time, best hiking seasons, type of trail terrain, what other trail users you may encounter, trail contacts (for updates on trail conditions), and trail schedules and usage fees.

No need for difficulty ratings since all hikes are "easy"—under 5 miles in length, minimal elevation gain, and relatively even terrain (except in the rainy season when most will be muddy).

The approximate hiking times are based on a standard hiking pace of 1.5 to 2 miles per hour, adjusted for terrain and reflecting normal trail conditions. The stated times will get you there and back, but be sure to add time for rest breaks and enjoying the trail's attractions. Although the stated times offer a planning guideline, you should gain a sense of your personal health, capabilities, and hiking style and make this judgment for yourself. If you're hiking with a group, add enough time for slower members. The amount of carried gear also will influence hiking speed. In all cases leave enough daylight to accomplish the task safely.

The **Finding the trailhead** section gives you dependable directions from a nearby city or town right down to where you'll want to park your car. The hike description is the meat of the chapter. Detailed and honest, it's the author's carefully researched impression of the trail. While it's impossible to cover everything, you can rest assured that we won't miss what's important. In **Miles and Directions** we provide mileage cues to key junctions and trail name changes, as well as points of interest. The selected benchmarks allow for a quick check on progress and serve as your touchstone for staying on course.

Most maps in this book indicate the general route of the hike. However, in some cases, the route is not well-defined so the map shows you how to reach the trailhead. In a couple cases, no map is necessary.

# How to Speak Hawaiian

The Hawaiian language has only twelve letters: the vowels a, e, i, o, and u, and the consonants h, k, l, m, n, p, and w. It also has a diacritical mark, the glottal stop (indicated by an apostrophe), that tells you how to separate the syllables. The apostrophe gives spoken Hawaiian its distinctive sound and rhythm. For example, chunky lava, *a'a,* is not pronounced "aaah," but "ah-ah." The word Hawai'i itself has a glottal stop, and you probably already know how to say it: "Howai-ee." If two vowels are not separated by a glottal stop, they are pronounced together, like the "ai" in Hawai'i.

Here are a few words you will hear over and over on Hawai'i. Many refer to physical features of the land and help interpret the names of significant landmarks:

*a'a* = rough, chunky lava
*aloha* = hello, good-by, love
*heiau* = holy place
*kapu* = taboo, forbidden, keep out
*kea* = white
*kokua* = please or help
*loa* = long
*lua* = hole or toilet

*mahalo* = thank you
*makai* = toward the sea
*mauka* = toward the mountain
*mauna* = mountain
*pahoehoe* = smooth, ropy lava
*pali* = cliff
*pu'u* = hill

# Maui Hike Ratings

All hikes in this guide are easy, but some are more strenuous than others. The list below rated hikes from easiest to most challenging.

**Easiest**
Kepaniwai Park Heritage Gardens (Hike 2)
Ke'anae Arboretum (Hike 10)
Tropical Gardens of Maui (Hike 3)
Garden of Eden (Hike 7)
'Iao Needle (Hike 1)
Sea Caves and Black Sand Beach (Hike 11)
Twin Falls (Hike 8)
Red Hill Summit Overlook (Hike 17)
'Ohe'o Gulch and the Seven Pools (Hike 13)
Waikamoi Ridge Nature Trail (Hike 9)
Hosmer Grove (Hike 15)
Nakalele Blowhole (Hike 5)
Ma'alaea Beach Walk (Hike 19)
Olowalu Petroglyphs (Hike 20)
Waihou Spring (Hike 6)
Waihe'e Valley (Swinging Bridges) (Hike 4)
Wai'anapanapa Coast Trail (Hike 12)
Pipiwai Trail (Hike 14)
Halemau'u Haleakala Overlook (Hike 16)
Into Haleakala Crater (Hike 18)
**Most Challenging**

# Map Legend

|  |  |
|---|---|
| ──⊂30⊃── | State Highway |
| ──────── | Local Road |
| ▬▬▬▬▬▬ | Featured Trail |
| ‑ ‑ ‑ ‑ ‑ ‑ | Trail |
| ∿∿∿ | River/Creek |
| ⬮ | Body of Water |
| ▤ | Local/State Park |
| ▤ | National Park |
| ✕ | Airport |
| ⌣ | Bridge |
| ‖‖‖‖‖‖‖‖ | Boardwalk/Steps |
| ∧ | Cavern/Cave/Natural Bridge |
| 🗼 | Lighthouse |
| 🄿 | Parking |
| ▲ | Peak |
| ■ | Point of Interest/Structure |
| ⌁ | Spring |
| ○ | Town |
| ⓫ | Trailhead |
| ▧ | Viewpoint/Overlook |
| ❓ | Visitor/Information Center |
| ⤳ | Waterfall |

# 1  'Iao Needle

Hike into the misty green forest at the western end of the island to one of Maui's most famous landmarks. 'Iao Needle is a lava spire thrusting up out of the dense, damp foliage lining the walls of a gorge sacred to native Hawaiians. King Kamehameha won a major victory at this site on his way to uniting the Hawaiian Islands. This hike is best in the morning before clouds and rain fill the valley.

**Distance:** 1 mile on interconnecting trails

**Elevation gain:** 100 feet

**Approximate hiking time:** 1 hour

**Trail surface:** Asphalt

**Seasons:** Year-round

**Other trail users:** None

**Canine compatibility:** Leashed dogs permitted

**Fees and permits:** None

**Schedule:** Open from 7:00 a.m. to 7:00 p.m. daily

**Map:** *USGS Wailuku*, but none needed

**Land status:** 'Iao Valley State Monument

**Trail contact:** Hawai'i State Parks; (808) 984-8109; www .hawaiistateparks.org

**Special considerations:** Stay on the path. You will see small use-trails that head off into the forest here and there, but these all lead onto private property where visitors are not welcome. Watch out for flash floods. Don't go wading along the stream when it's raining hard.

**Finding the trailhead:** From Kahului drive Highway 32 west through Wailuku, where the road becomes West Main Street. In the center of town, among government buildings, pass the junction with Highway 330 on the right (north), then pass Highway 30 on the left (south). Highway 32 becomes Highway 320 at a sign pointing straight ahead to 'Iao Needle. About 1 mile beyond reach a Y junc-

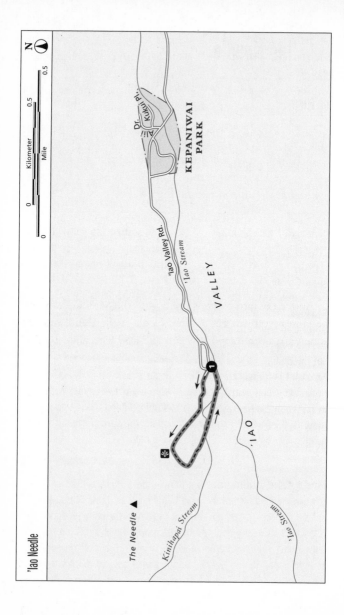

'Iao Needle

The Needle ▲

Kinihapai Stream

'Iao Stream

'Iao Stream

'IAO

VALLEY

'Iao Stream

'Iao Valley Rd.

KEPANIWAI PARK

Dr.

Kukui Pl.

Pl.

N

0    Kilometer    0.5

0    Mile    0.5

tion and follow the right fork for 4 miles, all the way to the end of the road and the parking lot. There are restrooms at the trailhead. **Trailhead GPS:** N20 52.51' / W56 32.43W'

## The Hike

Be sure to stop at the trailhead interpretive panels that explain the geologic and (sometimes bloody) human history of this sacred valley. The path begins at a showy red-orange flowered royal poinciana tree. You can choose any of a series of circular routes. The lowest one, the Lu'au Trail, is planted with species of plants brought to Hawai'i by the early Polynesians, including a terraced taro patch. Taro root is the source of *poi,* the starchy paste/glue that was the staple food of the early Hawaiians and is still cultivated and eaten today. You can find it at local supermarkets.

Above the taro patch is the trail to the Middle Lookout, the closest you can get to the Needle itself. You'll have to crane your neck to spot the top at 2,250 feet, almost 1,200 feet straight above you. The Kinihapai Stream tumbles down far, far below. You can leave the lookout and follow a third trail around the ridge separating Kinihapai and 'Iao Streams, and descend to skirt 'Iao Stream back to where the three paths meet. The two streams themselves meet below the parking lot.

# 2 Kepaniwai Park and Heritage Gardens

This walk follows a lovely winding path through gardens, ceremonial structures, and statuary celebrating the various cultures that have been stirred into the melting pot of present-day Hawai'i. There is a covered picnic area nearby and 'Iao Needle, which you should not miss, is just up the road.

**Distance:** 0.5-mile loop
**Elevation change:** Negligible
**Approximate hiking time:** 30 minutes
**Trail surface:** Asphalt
**Seasons:** Year-round
**Other trail users:** None
**Canine compatibility:** Dogs not permitted

**Fees and permits:** None
**Schedule:** Open from 7:00 a.m. to 7:00 p.m. daily
**Land status:** Maui County Park
**Map:** *USGS Wailuku,* but none needed
**Trail contact:** Maui Parks and Recreation; (808) 874-8137

**Finding the trailhead:** From Kahului drive Highway 32 west through Wailuku, where the road becomes West Main Street. In the center of town, among government buildings, pass the junction with Highway 330 on your right (north), then pass Highway 30 on your left (south). Highway 32 becomes Highway 320 at a sign pointing straight ahead to 'Iao Needle. About 1 mile beyond reach a Y intersection; follow the left fork for 2 miles to the gardens. Park on your left (south). There is a covered picnic area and restrooms near the parking area that are not always open. **Trailhead GPS:** N20 52.59' / W156 32.01'

## The Hike

Wander up the winding path in any direction you choose, walking beside pools of koi and crossing pretty bridges

# Kepaniwai Park and Heritage Gardens

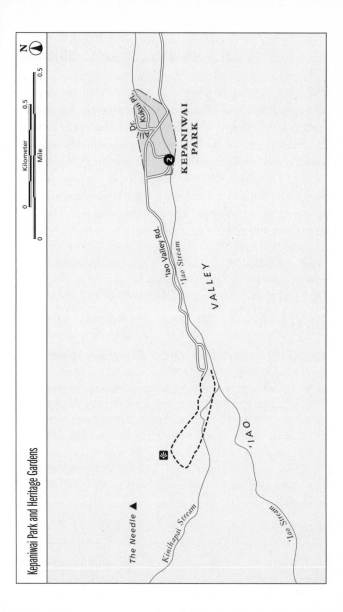

over a creek lined with showy tropical flowers. There is a Philippine *nipa* hut, an ornate Korean pagoda, a traditional Polynesian *hale* (house), a Japanese house, a Chinese temple, and a Portuguese dwelling with a great shady banyan tree at its center. There's also a prim little New England-style cottage from the time of the missionaries who came to "convert the heathen." Their descendents established the vast sugarcane plantations that blanketed the islands and recruited the Asian and Portuguese immigrants to work in the fields. The workers' lives were terribly hard: Some died and some returned home when their contracts expired, but many stayed to add their particular seasonings to the cultural stew that is Hawai'i.

The setting of this village is both serene and dramatic, tucked into a little notch near the mouth of the 'Iao Valley. In good weather the gardens are cozy, protected, and perfect for a picnic, with 'Iao Stream gurgling away in the background. On the other hand the mountains that enclose the area are high and dark and jagged at the top, and the river can become a raging torrent when it rains.

# 3 Tropical Gardens of Maui

Take an idyllic, shady stroll among a dazzling array of flowers, ferns, and trees from all over the tropical world. The three-acre site straddles both sides of 'Iao Stream, which you cross on a bridge. Other bridges pass over little brooks and cascades. If you come on a weekday, you'll have the place almost to yourself.

**Distance:** 1 mile
**Elevation change:** Negligible
**Approximate hiking time:** 1 to 2 hours
**Trail surface:** Asphalt
**Seasons:** Year-round
**Other trail users:** None
**Canine compatibility:** Dogs not permitted

**Fees and permits:** A small fee is charged
**Schedule:** Open from 9:00 a.m. to 5:00 p.m.
**Maps:** *USGS quad Wailuku;* trail guide provided at the entrance
**Trail contact:** Tropical Gardens of Maui; (808) 244-3085; www .tropicalgardensofmaui.com

**Finding the trailhead:** From Kahului drive Highway 32 west through Wailuku, where the road becomes West Main Street. In the center of town, among government buildings, pass the junction with Highway 330 on your right (north), then pass Highway 30 on your left (south). Highway 32 becomes Highway 320 at a sign pointing straight ahead to 'Iao Needle. About 1 mile beyond reach a Y intersection; follow the right fork for about 0.5 mile to the garden entrance on the right (north). There are restrooms and a small gift shop at the entrance. **Trailhead GPS:** N20 53.02' / W156 32.08'

## The Hike

This is like a journey all the way around the world. You'll walk among more kinds of plants than you dreamed existed,

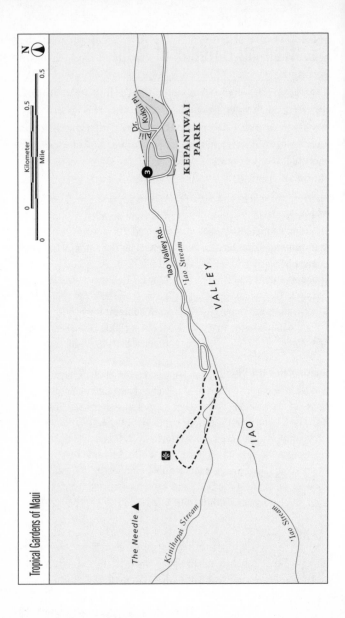

Tropical Gardens of Maui

N

The Needle ▲

Kinihapai Stream

'IAO

'Iao Stream

VALLEY

'Iao Stream

'Iao Valley Rd.

KEPANIWAI PARK

3

Dr.

Kukui Pl.

Kilometer    0.5

Mile        0.5

0

in colors you've never seen before. Orchids dangle from the branches and stems of larger plants that look like organisms from another planet. There are huge cycads, which look like a cross between a palm tree and a fern, primitive plants that appeared on the earth before Mother Nature even invented flowers. Dozens of varieties of palms—all different—mingle with splashy brilliant gingers and bromeliads that look like waxy flowers containing other, smaller flowers of a different color. Their stiff, cuplike leaves and bracts collect pools of water that support entire communities of animals, from insects to frogs.

You'll get a little trail guide when you enter the garden that points out some of the most interesting species, and many of the plants are labeled. But whether or not you are interested in what they are called, wandering among them provides a treat for all the senses.

# 4 Waihe'e Valley (Swinging Bridges)

The trail's informal name comes from the two suspension bridges that cross the Waihe'e River. The trail passes through private property belonging to the company that owns the irrigation ditch that in earlier days supplied water to sugarcane fields. The swinging bridges are fun to cross and there is a perfect little pool to swim in at the end. It's on the rainy side of the island, so the earlier in the day you go the better . . . but expect to get wet anyway.

**Distance:** 3.8 miles out and back

**Elevation gain:** 100 feet

**Approximate hiking time:** 1.5 to 2.5 hours

**Trail surface:** Part road; part good trail; sometimes rocky

**Seasons:** Year-round, except during heavy or steady rain

**Other trail users:** Cyclists

**Canine compatibility:** Leashed dogs permitted

**Fees and permits:** A small entrance fee is charged at a kiosk where you can buy sodas and snacks and sample macadamia nuts. The entrance fee pays for maintenance.

**Schedule:** Open from 9:00 a.m. to 5:00 p.m.

**Land status:** Private property

**Map**: USGS Wailuku, but the trail is not shown on the topo

**Trail contact:** Wailuku Agribusiness; (808) 244-9570

**Special considerations:** The valley is subject to flash flooding. Don't go in if it's raining.

**Finding the trailhead:** From Wailuku drive north on Highway 340 about 5 miles, through the little town of Waihe'e. About 1 mile beyond the town turn left (west) on Waihe'e Valley Road. Follow it about 0.5 mile to a T intersection. A sign directs you to the right. The road ends at a gate and a kiosk. Pit toilets near the entrance; cold drinks and snacks available at the kiosk. **Trailhead GPS:** N20 14.16' / W156 52.65'

# The Hike

Park in a wide spot just beyond the kiosk and hike up the road to a Y junction with chains across both forks. Step over the chain on the left fork. Soon you will begin to hear water flowing through the ditch on the left (south). At a second fork turn left again, stepping over or around another gate. The road levels out and you stroll alongside sugarcane and *laua'e* ferns to the first swinging bridge. It looks pretty rickety, but it's firm. At times there is very little water in the stream beneath the bridge because most has been diverted for irrigation, though it can run fast and deep if it's raining upstream.

As you continue you will notice irrigation ditches, some of them running through tunnels blasted through the lava, along with the machinery that opens and closes them. About 50 yards after the road turns into trail you come to the next swinging bridge and cross back to the other side of the stream. Now that you're above the place where the water gets diverted, there should be a moderate flow. Continue through a bamboo forest and cross the stream two times more. If the water is low enough you can cross on dry rocks. The wet ones are *very* slippery. You will pass a nice pool, but the best is yet to come.

Continue up a narrow rocky path/streambed beneath wild ginger that sometimes reaches higher than your head. As you draw nearer to the riverside you'll notice the river is full and roaring because you have passed another diversion ditch. It's also feeling more like wilderness. A short rise, then a short drop, takes you to the dam at trail's end, where a "waterfall" pours into a perfect diving pool. Upstream, clouds permitting, you can see where the valley widens a bit

# Waihe'e Valley (Swinging Bridges)

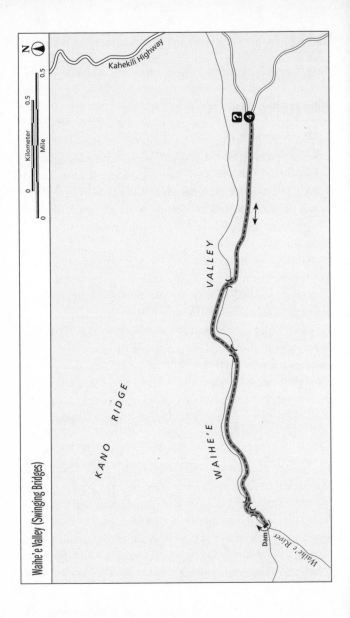

to reveal the phenomenally steep cliffs at its head, decorated with a narrow, long, vertical string of white waterfalls.

Return the same way.

## Miles and Directions

**0.0**  Entrance kiosk
**0.1**  First Y junction; take the left fork
**0.2**  Second Y junction; go left again
**1.9**  Swimming hole at the dam (N20 93.48' / W156 54.77')
**3.8**  Arrive back at the trailhead

# 5  Nakalele Blowhole

Blowholes are created when the sea undercuts a lava cliff in which there is a crack or other opening. When the surf crashes into the shore, the water is forced up through the hole like a geyser. The height of the fountain varies with the tides and the size of the surf, and it's especially fun to go when the tide is coming in and the water shoots higher and higher. There are blowholes on all the major islands—maybe some on the minor ones too—but the setting for the Nakahele Blowhole is arguably the most scenic of all, and it isn't surrounded by souvenir stands. On a weekday you'll only share the scene with a few goats, but summer weekends are busier.

**Distance:** 0.6 mile out and back
**Elevation loss:** 100 feet
**Approximate hiking time:** 1 hour
**Trail surface:** Lava rock; sometimes slippery, sometimes jagged
**Seasons:** Year-round
**Other trail users:** None
**Canine compatibility:** Dogs permitted
**Fees and permits:** None
**Schedule:** Safest during daylight hours

**Land status:** Private
**Map:** *USGS Napili,* but you don't really need a map
**Trail contact:** None
**Special considerations:** Watch your step and, especially, watch your children. There really isn't a defined trail, the rocks can be slippery and sharp, and the surf is dangerous. Do not stand too close to the blowhole!

**Finding the trailhead:** From Lahaina or Ka'anapali drive Highway 30 north and east to milepost 38 and watch for a parking area on the *makai* (ocean) side. From Wailuku, drive Highway 340 west and north, including a section of winding one lane road, to where the route becomes Highway 30. Pull out near milepost 38 in the parking area on the right (*makai*/ocean side). There are no facilities of any kind here. Leave nothing in your car. **Trailhead GPS:** N21 01.42' / W156 35.40'

## The Hike

Several informal routes lead from the highway to the blowhole. The easiest way to find the blowhole is to start down the orange-gated road over windswept, goat-mowed ground, and wander downhill to the right (southeast) toward the lighthouse. Along the way you'll see hundreds—maybe thousands—of stacked lava rock cairns. Making cairns is a tourist tradition, not a native Hawaiian one.

As you near the lighthouse (actually, there is no house, just a light) you'll see a small area enclosed with a wire fence. Below that you can see the top of a ladder sticking up from the cliff edge. (You don't have to use it. It's just a reference point.) Below are some of the world's most beautiful tide pools, wonderful places to explore *very carefully* at low tide. To continue on to the blowhole, pass to the right (south) of the light to a gully where white paint splashed on the rocks marks the easiest route. The fabulous, eerie sculptures and patterns in the eroded lava make this worth a trip even if there were no blowhole at the end. Be careful, though. The lava is very sharp and a slip could cause a nasty gash. Stop now and then to enjoy the stunning views to the south across Honokohau Bay to the jutting fin-shaped rock called Kahakuloa Head.

You will be able to hear the intermittent roar and whoosh of the blowhole as you cross a low flat area, then you'll see the blowhole itself shooting a fountain of water out of the middle of a flat terrace downhill and to the right

(northeast). When you can tear yourself away, just head back uphill toward the highway, keeping slightly to the right (west).

## Miles and Directions

**0.0**  Start
**0.3**  Blowhole (N21 01.47' / W156 35.20')
**0.6**  Arrive back at the trailhead

# 6 Waihou Spring

This hike in cool upcountry Maui takes you through an experimental forest of pines planted by the U.S. Geological Service and Hawaii's Division of Forestry and Wildlife. The spring itself is usually dry, unless it has very recently rained, but the setting is pretty anytime. It is an easy, fairly level loop with an optional short but very steep side trip down to the spring—not difficult if you take your time.

**Distance:** 2.1 miles round-trip, including side trip to the spring
**Elevation change:** 500 feet
**Approximate hiking time:** 1 to 2 hours
**Trail surface:** Mostly dirt road; some narrow trail
**Seasons:** Year-round
**Other trail users:** None
**Canine compatibility:** Leashed dogs permitted
**Fees and permits:** None

**Schedule:** Open sunrise to sunset
**Land status:** Waihou Spring Forest Reserve
**Map:** *USGS Kilohana*
**Trail contact:** Hawai'i Department of Land and Natural Resources; (808) 873-3508; www.hawaiitrails.org
**Special considerations:** Deep shade along the route makes collecting/reading some GPS coordinates impossible.

**Finding the trailhead:** From the Kahului Airport take Highway 36 (the Hana Highway) for 6 miles to Pa'ia. At the signal at Baldwin Avenue (Highway 390), turn right (*mauka,* toward the mountain). Go 7 miles on Baldwin Avenue to Makawao, and continue straight through town to where Baldwin Avenue becomes Baldwin-Olinda, then just Olinda Road (Highway 390). Wind up this narrow lane for another 5 miles, passing the Maui Bird Conservation Center, to the signed trailhead on the right (south). Do not leave anything in your car. **Trailhead GPS:** N20 48.22' / W156 16.48'

# The Hike

Go around a gate and through a hikers' entrance to wander down a wide needle-strewn road between regular rows of pines. At a junction about 0.1 mile along, a sign keeps you pointed straight ahead (south). Descend gradually, dipping into a gully in a grove of ash trees. Just beyond, another sign marks the beginning of the loop part of the hike. Turn right (west), starting the loop in a counterclockwise direction.

Occasional redwoods join the pines and ash trees. A few steps beyond the point where the redwoods appear, a sign directs you to right (north) toward the overlook and the spring. There is a bench at the overlook, which doesn't overlook much of anything as the forest is so dense. To get down to the spring, continue on down the steep switchbacks that can be slippery when wet. A sign marks the end of the trail.

The location of the spring is pretty even if it isn't flowing since it comes out of a lava cliff hung with ferns and honeycombed with niches and holes. It is dry these days because its water has been diverted, first for sugar growing, later for development. Go slowly and carefully back up the switchbacks to the overlook, turn left (south) to return to the junction where you left the loop part of the trail, then go right (south) to complete the loop. At the close of the loop, turn right (north), and follow the lollipop stick back to your car.

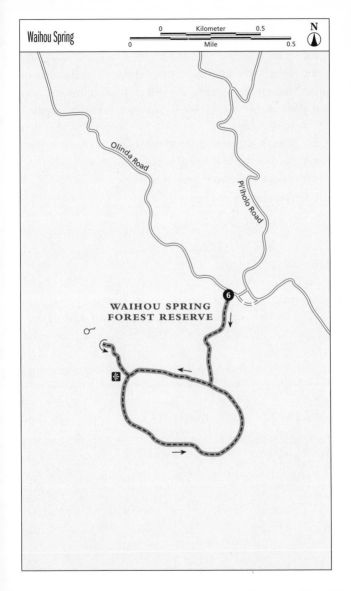

Waihou Spring

Kilometer

Mile

N

Olinda Road

Pi'iholo Road

WAIHOU SPRING
FOREST RESERVE

6

## Miles and Directions

**0.0** Start

**0.1** Road cuts off left (east); continue straight ahead

**0.3** Turn right (west) starting the loop

**0.6** Reach the turnoff to overlook and spring, turn slightly right (northwest)

**1.0** Climb steeply down to the spring

**1.4** Return to the loop, turn right (south)

**1.8** Close the loop, turning right (north)

**2.1** Arrive back at trailhead

# 7 Garden of Eden

This commercial botanical garden and arboretum sprawls over twenty-six acres and includes some bonus features like a view of a spectacular waterfall you can't see from anywhere else.

**Distance:** 2.5 miles round-trip
**Elevation change:** None, unless you go to the base of the waterfall
**Approximate hiking time:** 1 to 2 hours
**Trail surface:** Well-groomed trail, though it's steep down to the waterfall
**Seasons:** Year-round
**Other trail users:** None
**Canine compatibility:** Dogs not permitted

**Fees and permits:** An entry fee is charged
**Schedule:** Open from 8:00 a.m. to 3:00 p.m. daily; closed during heavy rain
**Maps:** *USGS Keanae;* trail guide provided at the entrance
**Trail contact:** Garden of Eden (Maui Botanical Gardens & Arboretum); (808) 572-9899; www .mauigardenofeden.com

**Finding the trailhead:** From Kahului drive to mile marker 10.5 on Highway 360 (the Hana Highway). Turn *mauka* (toward the mountain) into the driveway and on to the entrance kiosk. You'll find restrooms, picnic areas, and a gift shop in the gardens. **Trailhead GPS** (estimate): N20 54.52' / W156 15.18'

## The Hike

A series of trails that you can wander along in any direction you like winds through clumps of tropical trees and flowers. Enjoy a spectacular view of Puohokamoa Falls from above that you won't get anywhere else, except perhaps from the air. There is a pretty water lily pool, as well as an area where ducks and peacocks hang out for kids to feed and a collection of macaws and cockatoos that will pose for photos with you. If you look far down the valley from the lily pond, almost to the sea, you can catch a glimpse of Keopuka Rock jutting out into the ocean. If it looks familiar, you might recognize it from the opening scene of *Jurassic Park,* as you will be told time and again.

A covered picnic area, toilets, gallery, and gift shop making the Garden of Eden a nice compromise between the hokey luau scene and real wilderness. You don't have to worry about somebody breaking into your car either. If you have good shoes, a sense of adventure, and don't mind getting muddy, you can follow a steep side trail about 0.5 mile down to the falls for a swim in the pool.

Barnes & Noble Booksellers #2276
325 Keawe #101
Lahaina, HI 96761
(808) 662-1300

STR:2276 REG:005 TRN:0384 CSHR:Joan W

BARNES & NOBLE MEMBER       EXP: 12/17/2015

Top Trails: Maui: Must-Do Hikes for Ever
  9780899976259        T1
  (1 @ 17.95) Member Card 10% (1.80)
  (1 @ 16.15)                      16.15
Best Easy Day Hikes Hawaii: Maui
  9780762743483        T1
  (1 @ 9.95) Member Card 10% (1.00)
  (1 @ 8.95)                        8.95

Subtotal                          25.10
Sales Tax T1 (4.167%)              1.05
TOTAL                             26.15
AMEX                              26.15
  Card#:   XXXXXXXXXXXX1003
  Expdate: XX/XX
  Auth:    566081
  Entry Method: Swiped

MEMBER SAVINGS                     2.80

Thanks for shopping at
Barnes & Noble

101.37A              12/08/2015 12:44PM

CUSTOMER COPY

and audio books made within 14 days of purchase from a Barnes & Noble store or Barnes & Noble.com with the below exceptions:

A store credit for the purchase price will be issued (i) for purchases made by check less than 7 days prior to the date of return, (ii) when a gift receipt is presented within 60 days of purchase, (iii) for textbooks, (iv) when the original tender is PayPal, or (v) for products purchased at Barnes & Noble College bookstores that are listed for sale in the Barnes & Noble Booksellers inventory management system.

Opened music CDs, DVDs, vinyl records, audio books may not be returned, and can be exchanged only for the same title and only if defective. NOOKs purchased from other retailers or sellers are returnable only to the retailer or seller from which they are purchased, pursuant to such retailer's or seller's return policy. Magazines, newspapers, eBooks, digital downloads, and used books are not returnable or exchangeable. Defective NOOKs may be exchanged at the store in accordance with the applicable warranty.

Returns or exchanges will not be permitted (i) after 14 days or without receipt or (ii) for product not carried by Barnes & Noble or Barnes & Noble.com.

*Policy on receipt may appear in two sections.*

## Return Policy

With a sales receipt or Barnes & Noble.com packing slip, a full refund in the original form of payment will be issued from any Barnes & Noble Booksellers store for returns of undamaged NOOKs, new and unread books, and unopened and undamaged music CDs, DVDs, vinyl records, toys/games and audio books made within 14 days of purchase from a Barnes & Noble Booksellers store or Barnes & Noble.com with the below exceptions:

A store credit for the purchase price will be issued (i) for purchases made by check less than 7 days prior to the date of return, (ii) when a gift receipt is presented within 60 days of purchase, (iii) for textbooks, (iv) when the original tender is PayPal, or (v) for products purchased at Barnes & Noble College bookstores that are listed for sale in the Barnes & Noble Booksellers inventory management system.

Opened music CDs, DVDs, vinyl records, audio books may not be returned, and can be exchanged only for the same title and only if defective. NOOKs purchased from other retailers or sellers are

# YOU MAY ALSO LIKE....

they are purchased, pursuant to such retailer's or seller's return policy. Magazines, newspapers, eBooks, digital downloads, and used books are not returnable or exchangeable. Defective NOOKs may be exchanged at the store in accordance with the applicable warranty.

Returns or exchanges will not be permitted (i) after 14 days or without receipt or (ii) for product not carried by Barnes & Noble or Barnes & Noble.com.

*Policy on receipt may appear in two sections.*

## Return Policy

With a sales receipt or Barnes & Noble.com packing slip, a full refund in the original form of payment will be issued from any Barnes & Noble Booksellers store for returns of undamaged NOOKs, new and unread books, and unopened and undamaged music CDs, DVDs, vinyl records, toys/games and audio books made within 14 days of purchase from a Barnes & Noble Booksellers store or Barnes & Noble.com with the below exceptions:

# 8 Twin Falls

Don't expect solitude on this very popular hike because the swimming is great and the falls are beautiful. It isn't exactly unspoiled wilderness, and it isn't even marked on the road, but everybody knows where it is. There's a little fruit and drink stand at the entrance and a jar for donations to help maintain the place. It has been closed at times because the path goes right past people's homes. Please stay on the trail, away from private property, and don't trash somebody else's neighborhood.

**Distance:** 1.4 miles out and back
**Elevation change:** Minimal
**Approximate hiking time:** 1 hour to most of the day
**Trail surface:** Part gravel road; part worn lava trail; part in the stream
**Seasons:** Year-round
**Other trail users:** None
**Canine compatibility:** Open to friendly dogs, even off leash

**Fees and permits:** None
**Schedule:** Daylight hours
**Map:** *USGS Paia,* but none needed
**Trail contact:** None
**Special considerations:** The stream can be very dangerous in heavy rain. The narrow valley is subject to flash floods that could sweep you away in an instant. Stay away in bad weather.

**Finding the trailhead:** From Kahului drive east on Highway 36 toward Hana for about 6 miles to the funky old ex-sugar mill/art colony/hippie haven town of Pa'ia. Continue for another 4 miles, to where Highway 36 becomes Highway 360 (the Hana Highway). Just past mile marker 2, and just before you cross a bridge over Ho'olawa Stream, look for a small parking shoulder and lots of activity on the right (*mauka/*toward the mountain) side of the road. There is no sign. Snacks available at the fruit stand. **Trailhead GPS:** N20 54.42' / W156 14.33'

# The Hike

Go through the gate, passing a little farm stand with fresh fruit and a pot for donations to help maintain the area. Begin walking down the gravel road, avoiding lots of minor roads to side trails that lead to little pools along Ho'olawa Stream, and others that are driveways to private residences. The road is lined with wonderful vegetation, including huge elephant ears called *ape* in Hawaiian (pronounced "ah-pay"), and appropriately named *Monstera deliciosa,* with leaves that have Swiss cheese holes in them.

At 0.5 mile a Y split is marked by a painted rock whose colors are faded and chipped. Both forks of the trail take you to waterfalls. If you want to keep your feet dry, follow the right (south) fork. Cross an irrigation ditch in a tangled *hau* forest, then walk along the retaining wall that separates the ditch from the stream itself. You'll have to step over a concrete block with a pipe on it that looks like the end of the ditch wall, but it actually keeps going. Where the wall ends at a big old banyan tree continue straight a few more yards, picking your way over roots and rocks to a fall pouring over a ferny lava cliff into a deep pool. Kids love to make the 25-foot leap from the top of the fall into the swimming hole.

To see the other waterfall, return to the painted rock and follow the left (southeast) fork until you reach another stream with a ditch running parallel to it. You'll have to wade from here. You can walk along the top of the wall separating stream from ditch for perhaps 50 yards, or just wade up the middle of the stream. The rocks underfoot are round and smooth and slippery, but it's not much more than knee-deep. Keep your camera or anything else that can't get wet wrapped in plastic in case you slip. The left-hand fall

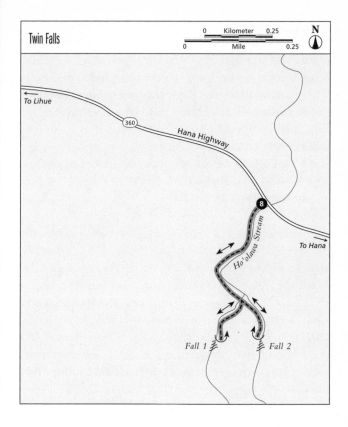

is higher than the other—perhaps 50 feet—and the water flows over a deep fern grotto. The pool is deep enough for swimming. Retrace your steps to the painted rock, and from there back to your car.

# Miles and Directions

**0.0**   Start at the gate

**0.5**   Painted rock junction; there are waterfalls both to the left (southeast) and right (south). Take your pick or visit both.

**0.6**   Reach the highest waterfall on the left fork (N20 54.17' / W156 14.62')

**0.8**   Reach the second fall

**0.9**   Return to the painted rock junction and retrace your path toward the trailhead.

**1.4**   Arrive back at the trailhead

# 9 Waikamoi Ridge Nature Trail

This is a good place to stretch your legs on the long road to Hana. It involves a steep climb, but is very short. It goes through magnificent old forest with views of Waikamoi Stream and the ocean. Take mosquito repellent.

**Distance:** 1 mile out and back
**Elevation gain:** 240 feet
**Approximate hiking time:** 45 minutes to 1 hour
**Trail surface:** Part gravel path; part worn lava with some slick tree roots
**Seasons:** Year-round
**Other trail users:** None
**Canine compatibility:** Leashed dogs permitted

**Fees and permits:** None required
**Schedule:** Sunrise to sunset
**Land status:** Hawai'i Division of Forestry and Wildlife
**Maps:** *USGS Keanae;* there's also a map at the trailhead but you don't really need one
**Trail contact:** Hawai'i Division of Forestry and Wildlife; (808) 984-8100; www.hawaiitrails.org

**Finding the trailhead:** From Kahului follow Highway 36 (the Hana Highway) eastward. A bit beyond 10 miles Highway 36 becomes Highway 360 and the numbers on the mileposts start over again. Continue to milepost 9.5, to a parking area on the *mauka* (toward the mountain) side of the road. There's a sign and there will be other cars. There are no facilities of any kind here. **Trailhead GPS:** N20 52.28' / W156 11.08'

## The Hike

The sheer size of the trees along the trail will leave you gasping. This is a nature trail and many of the big trees are labeled. You might be surprised to discover that most of them are kinds of eucalyptus . . . but eucalyptus bigger

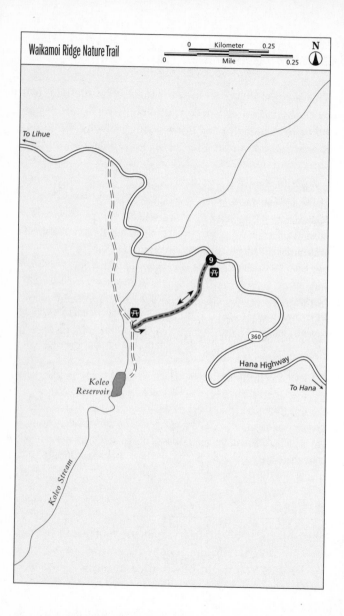

Waikamoi Ridge Nature Trail

0          Kilometer          0.25

0                Mile              0.25

**N**

To Lihue

Koleo Reservoir

Koleo Stream

360

Hana Highway

To Hana

9

than you ever imagined. The vines climbing up into their branches, sometimes completely covering the trunks, should also seem familiar, but they are also so large you might not recognize them as ordinary houseplants. Among them are philodendron and pothos, whose leaves are the size of umbrellas. Among the deep greens are startling red bunches of heliconias. You can see how they earned their common name of lobster claws.

Climb on a terraced gravel path, past a sign warning QUIET. TREES AT WORK, to a covered picnic area with a barbecue overlooking the sea. The gravel path ends at 0.3 mile, but the route continues upward to the right (west) on sometimes slippery rocks and tree roots. Enter a forest of bamboo, *ti,* and *hala,* picking your way carefully over slippery roots. Just as the trail Ts into an overgrown dirt road, you'll arrive at a grassy flat with another covered picnic table. This one overlooks a valley that is a sea of waving bamboo, below which is the real ocean. This is the end of the trail. Return the way you came.

# 10  Ke'anae Arboretum

This is an easy stroll along a stream through a garden of trees and flowers from all over the tropical world. The trail meanders gently up a series of broad terraces originally built by native Hawaiians for growing taro. The lower portion is planted with exotic trees, while the upper end is devoted to plants introduced and used by the ancient Polynesians. It's a perfect opportunity to take a break from concentrating on the winding Hana Highway; you can stretch your legs and even splash in the stream.

**Distance:** 1 mile out and back
**Elevation change:** Negligible
**Approximate hiking time:** 1 hour or less
**Trail surface:** Asphalt road narrowing to smooth trail
**Other trail users:** None
**Canine compatibility:** Dogs not permitted
**Seasons:** Year-round

**Fees and permits:** None
**Land status:** Hawai'i Department of Land and Natural Resources
**Map:** *USGS Keanae,* but a map is not required
**Trail contact:** Hawai'i Department of Land and Natural Resources; (808) 984-8100; www.hawaiitrails.org

**Finding the trailhead:** From Kahului drive Highway 36 to Highway 360 (the Hana Highway) to a sharp bend at about mile marker 17. The arboretum is on your right (*mauka*/toward the mountain), where there is some parking, but there is more space across the road on the *makai* (toward the ocean) side. There are no facilities of any kind here, but there are toilets a short distance back (northward) up the road at the Kaumahina State Wayside rest area. Bring your own picnic, as well as your mosquito repellent. **Trailhead GPS:** N20 51.30' / W156 08.57'

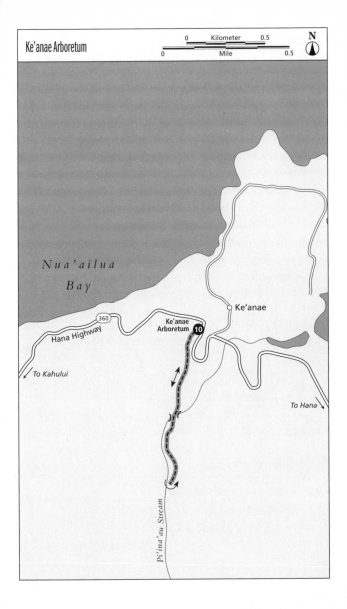

Ke'anae Arboretum

Nua'ailua
Bay

360

Hana Highway

Ke'anae
Arboretum  10

Ke'anae

To Kahului

To Hana

Pi'ina'au Stream

# The Hike

Go past the gate and down the broad asphalt path lined with the ubiquitous red and white impatiens that thrive in damp places all over Hawai'i. The Pi'ina'au Stream is noisy but invisible at first, then appears from behind a dense patch of ginger. You will follow it the rest of the way. As the ground levels out a wide lawn begins, dotted with clumps of palms and other tropical trees with identifying labels. Even if botany leaves you cold, there are wondrous things to see here: teak trees with impossibly enormous leaves, and dozens of kinds of eucalyptus, including the painted gum with beautiful multicolored pink, green, yellow, and purple stripes running down its trunk. Some of the forest giants have huge sculptural prop roots or buttresses flowing out along the ground in wavy patterns like the train of a bridal gown. There are also showy patches of red torch ginger and heliconias (also known as lobster claws).

At 0.3 mile the asphalt ends and you come to a collection of plants brought here and used by the native Hawaiians: papaya, coconut, breadfruit, *noni,* wild yam, *ti,* taro, and paper mulberry, which was used to make *tapa* cloth.

Follow the stream back the way you came when you have had enough.

## Miles and Directions

- **0.0**  Ke'anae Arboretum entrance
- **0.5**  Maintained trail ends
- **1.0**  Arrive back at the trailhead

# 11 Sea Caves and Black Sand Beach

This short tour explores several natural wonders created when flowing molten lava meets the sea. The coastline is classic Hawai'i: picture-postcard pretty with swaying palms and turquoise sea. It is also the setting of a romantic—and tragic—Hawaiian myth.

**Distance:** 0.4-mile modified loop

**Elevation loss:** 40 feet

**Approximate hiking time:** 30 to 40 minutes

**Trail surface:** Lava, asphalt, and sand

**Seasons:** Year-round

**Other trail users:** None

**Canine compatibility:** Dogs not permitted

**Fees and permits:** None

**Schedule:** Parking lot gate is open Monday through Friday from 7:00 a.m. to 6:00 p.m.; weekends and holidays from 8:00 a.m. to 6:00 p.m.

**Land Status:** Wai'anapanapa State Park

**Map:** *USGS Hana*, but a map is not really needed

**Trail contact:** Hawai'i Department of Land and Natural Resources; (808) 984-8109; www.hawaiistateparks.org

**Finding the trailhead:** From either Kahului or Hana drive to mile marker 32 on Highway 360 (the Hana Highway), where a sign points *makai* (toward the sea) to Wai'anapanapa State Park. Drive about 0.5 mile down the narrow park road to a T intersection. Turn left (north) toward the campground and park at road's end. There are toilets and water at the campground. Do not leave valuables in your car. **Trailhead GPS:** N20 47.14' / W156 00.07'

# The Hike

A sign at the parking lot directs you to the left, where an interpretive panel tells one of several versions of the story of a Hawaiian princess who was killed by her jealous husband. Now and then the water at the base of the sea cave turns red with her blood, according to the myth . . . or with a bloom of aquatic life, according to biologists.

Descend on lava stairs just a few yards to the first cave on the right. The caves are the remains of a lava tube whose roof has collapsed in places. The walls above are hung with ferns and other deep green tropical foliage, and the cave itself is properly dark and drippy and mysterious. When you emerge from the other end, the path is bright with cheerful begonias and impatiens. The intricate pattern of branches arching overhead are created by a native Hawaiian shrub called *hau,* often planted as natural fencing. (You can see why: "*Hau* will I ever get to the other side?") Its flowers are bright yellow with purple centers, fading to deep orange with dark centers when they fall, still beautiful. A few steps up bring you to a short spur to the left and a gorgeous view of the bay. Skirt the edge of the second cave, then ascend a few more steep stairs to close the loop. There is another spectacular viewpoint behind a railing at the top.

Back at the fork at the trail's beginning where you turned left to see the cave, you now turn right instead and descend another steep path curving down toward the beach. There is a veritable forest of warning signs here, all of which you should take very seriously, most having to do with

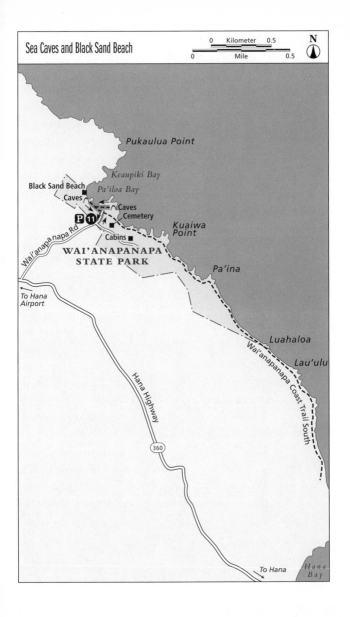

swimming in the little cove ahead. Accidents due to tricky currents and unexpected waves have been all too frequent. The beach at the bottom is small and usually crowded unless you're there early or late in the day. The black sand is coarse and sharp and hard on bare feet.

Once you're down on the beach, follow the rock face around to the right for just a few feet, where you will find a tunnel in the cliff that goes about 25 yards clear through to the ocean. Be careful! The water can rush in with great force, smash you against the walls or suck you out to sea. Return the way you came.

# 12  Wai'anapanapa Coast Trail

This hike follows a shoreline of incomparable beauty, with dozens of blowholes and sea arches, fascinating lava formations, archeological sites, and possible sightings of sea turtles and dolphins. The route goes all the way to Hana, but beyond the first mile the way is rough, indistinct, and dangerous if you aren't very, very careful. The hike described here goes about 1 mile out and back, and includes the most exciting part of the coast.

**Distance:** 2 miles out and back
**Elevation change:** Negligible
**Approximate hiking time:** 45 minutes to 1.5 hours
**Trail surface:** Fairly smooth lava at first, rougher *a'a* as you progress
**Seasons:** Year-round
**Other trail users:** None
**Canine compatibility:** Dogs not permitted
**Fees and permits:** None
**Schedule:** Parking lot gate is open Monday through Friday from 7:00 a.m. to 6:00 p.m.; weekends and holidays from 8:00 a.m. to 6:00 p.m.
**Map:** *USGS Hana*
**Trail contact:** Hawai'i Department of Land and Natural Resources; (808) 984-8109; www.hawaiistateparks.org
**Schedule:** Parking lot gate is open Monday through Friday, 7:00 a.m. to 6:00 p.m.; weekends and holidays from 8:00 a.m. to 6:00 p.m.

**Finding the trailhead:** From either Kahului or Hana drive to mile marker 32 on Highway 360 (the Hana Highway); only about 3.5 miles north of Hana). A sign points *makai* (toward the sea) to Wai'anapanapa State Park. Drive about 0.5 miles down the narrow park road to a T intersection. Turn left (north) toward the campground and park in the lot at road's end. There are toilets and water at the campground. Do not leave valuables in your car. **Trailhead GPS:** N20 47.15' / W156 00.07'

## The Hike

From the parking lot take the short concrete sidewalk straight toward the ocean and sea arch overlook. Turn right (southeast) onto an asphalt trail, passing the picnic area, then the old cemetery with the campground behind it. At the CAUTION WATCH YOUR STEP sign leave the asphalt path, which winds back up to the caretaker's house, and go left down the dirt path toward the ocean. There's a picture of hikers to show the trail.

Pass another section of the cemetery, then skirt the cliff edge through *hala* and *naupaka,* passing below the state park cabins. The coast is spectacular, but take a moment to examine low seaside shrubs with succulent leaves and white flowers that look as though they have been cut in half. Hawaiian legend has it that a beautiful maiden became angry at her lover, tore one of the flowers in half, and told him she would not forgive him until he found the other half and brought it back to her. He failed in his search and died of a broken heart.

The footing from here on consists of uneven chunks of lava. The ground shakes and thunders beneath your feet when the surf is up. Beyond the cabins you'll reach a wide spot in the trail where hissing and rumbling tells you there is a blowhole nearby. When the tide is in, you are likely to get wet with its spray. From here on you will pass one blowhole after another, one sea arch after another, until at about 0.5 mile you cross over a lava tube on a lava bridge where the sea rushes in beneath you with every wave.

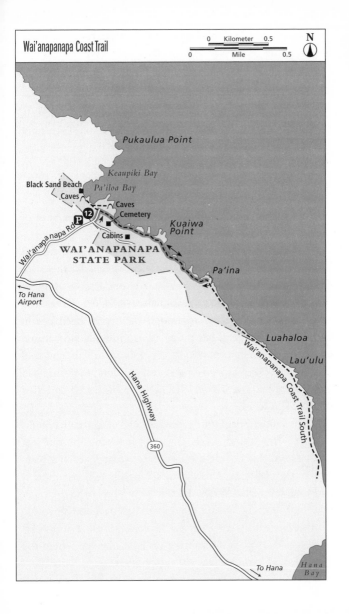

A few stair steps hacked out of the lava take you down to a pebbly cove. When you climb out you come to the remains of a *heiau,* or Hawaiian temple. Beyond that you pass through a sort of portal to an overlook with a bench. At the end of the first mile a road heads off to the right (west) in a grassy spot, heading back up toward the highway and the Hana School. This is the place to turn around. Don't forget to watch for dolphins and sea turtles offshore.

The route continues for more than 3 miles, all the way to Hana Bay, but it becomes much more obscure and difficult— and you have seen the best by now anyway. Return as you came.

## Miles and Directions

**0.0**  Start

**1.0**  Turnaround point (N20 46.40' / W155 59.30')

**2.0**  Arrive back at the parking lot

# 13 'Ohe'o Gulch and the Seven Pools

The Seven "Sacred" Pools are the most popular attraction at this end of Maui. There are more than seven pools, depending on where you begin your count, and there is nothing sacred about any of them. (The name was an invention of the tourist industry.) Still, the setting is beautiful, with Pipiwai Stream flowing down 'Ohe'o Gulch, dropping over one waterfall after another, into one lovely pool after another. The last several of these pools, just before the stream flows into the ocean, are perfect for swimming.

**Distance:** 0.5-mile loop
**Elevation gain:** 80 feet
**Approximate hiking time:** 30 to 40 minutes, not counting time out for swimming
**Trail surface:** Mostly asphalt
**Seasons:** Year-round, except just after a big rainstorm
**Other trail users:** None
**Canine compatibility:** Dogs not permitted
**Fees and permits:** No permit needed. A national park entrance fee is charged.
**Schedule:** Year-round, though not after a heavy storm

**Land status:** Haleakala National Park
**Map:** *USGS Hana,* but a map isn't really needed
**Trail contact:** Kipahulu Visitor Center; (808)248-7375; www.nps.gov/hale
**Special considerations:** Pipiwai Stream flows down a narrow gorge that makes it subject to flash flooding. Check at the visitor center to make sure conditions are safe, and heed all park service warning signs. Do not swim in the ocean in this area. The shore is rugged and rocky and the currents deadly.

**Finding the trailhead:** From Hana drive 10 miles south and west on Highway 31, past the boundary of Haleakala National Park, and across the bridge over 'Ohe'o Gulch. Turn left *(makai/*toward the sea)

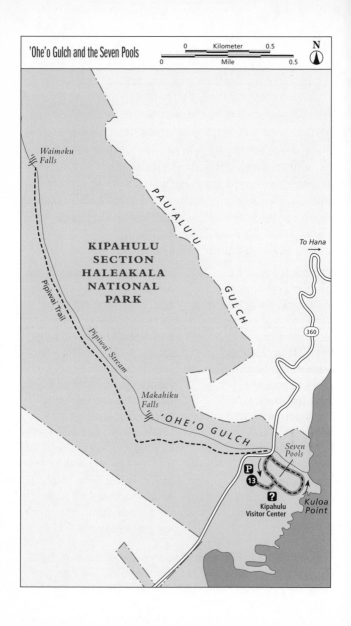

'Ohe'o Gulch and the Seven Pools

Kilometer
0          0.5
Mile
0          0.5

N

Waimoku
Falls

PAU'ALU'U GULCH

KIPAHULU
SECTION
HALEAKALA
NATIONAL
PARK

To Hana

360

Pipiwai Trail

Pipiwai Stream

Makahiku
Falls

'OHE'O GULCH

Seven
Pools

P
13

Kuloa
Point

Kipahulu
Visitor Center

into the Kipahulu Visitor Center parking lot. (*Note:* Highway 360—the Hana Highway coming from Kahului—ends at Hana. It becomes Highway 31 as it continues south.) There are restrooms at the parking lot and water in the visitor center. **Trailhead GPS:** N 20 39.43' / W156 02.28'

## The Hike

From the parking lot, walk straight toward the ocean and the visitor center until you reach a big trail sign, where you turn left (west). Just beyond is a model of a traditional Hawaiian house with information panels telling about how it was constructed. Beyond that you will reach a Y junction. Follow the right fork (marked TRAIL) and walk beneath an overarching canopy of *kukui* nut trees and a big banyan tree with hundreds of aerial roots reaching down to the ground to form new trunks. Emerge, blinking, into sunshine, where the path curves gently to the left, passing an ancient burial site. You can cut off the main trail here and walk a few yards toward the cliff above the sea for a look at the wild coastline, then return to the path and follow the asphalt steps down to the pools.

Unless you have arrived fairly early in the morning, at least before 9:00 a.m., you'll find yourself part of a crowd. This is, understandably, a very popular place. The asphalt trail continues uphill, passing spur trails down to the pools. There are interpretive panels along the way explaining the geologic origin of the pools. Continue upward along the stream almost to the highway, where a sign directs you to the left (south), back toward the ranger station, to complete the counterclockwise loop.

# 14  Pipiwai Trail

This is the best day hike on Maui. It takes you up alongside Pipiwai Stream, first through a guava orchard, then through a magical, musical bamboo forest, and on to an enchanting pool at the base of Waimoku Falls. Try to go early in the morning so you can savor the place in solitude.

**Distance:** 3.6 miles out and back

**Elevation gain:** 800 feet

**Approximate hiking time:** 3 to 4 hours

**Trail surface:** Worn lava, often muddy, with large tree roots across the trail; two rock-hopping stream crossings

**Seasons:** Year-round, though not after a heavy rain

**Other trail users:** None

**Canine compatibility:** Dogs not permitted

**Fees and permits:** No permit required. Kipahulu is the coastal extension of Haleakala National Park. You can pay your park entrance fee at the visitor center.

**Schedule:** Sunrise to sunset

**Land status:** Haleakala National Park

**Map:** *USGS Hana*

**Trail contact:** Kipahulu Visitor Center; (808) 248-7375; www .nps.gov/hale

**Special considerations:** Pipiwai Stream flows down a narrow gorge that makes it subject to flash floods when there is heavy rain in the mountains. Check at the visitor center to make sure conditions are safe before you set out. Also heed the signs advising hikers against jumping into the stream from the rocks above. There have been many, many injuries here.

**Finding the trailhead:** From Hana drive 10 miles south then west on Highway 31, past the boundary of Haleakala National Park and across the bridge over Pipiwai Stream. Turn left (*makai/*toward the ocean) into the Kipahulu Visitor Center parking lot. (*Note:* Highway 360—the Hana Highway from Kahului—ends at Hana. It becomes

Highway 31 as it continues south.) There is an official trailhead with a large sign to the right (north) of the parking lot, or you can cross the street from the parking lot, turn right (west), and follow the trail that parallels the road for a few yards to where it turns left *(mauka/* toward the mountain). There are restrooms at the parking lot and bottled water available at the visitor center. **Trailhead GPS:** N20 39.50' / W156 02.37'

## The Hike

The trail follows the edge of the cliff above Pipiwai Stream among mountain apple and guava trees, both of which produce delicious fruit in spring and summer. Picking your way over tangles of roots, climb past several openings in the dense vegetation leading to trail spurs from which you can watch cascades tumble into pools below. In about 0.5 mile you reach a lava-walled overlook to Makahiku Falls, 184 feet high. The waterfall can be spectacular or just a trickle, depending on recent weather. Do not try to climb down the cliff to get the falls.

Pass through a gate, closing it behind you, and begin to climb more steeply, passing a huge old mango tree, and beyond that a truly awesome banyan tree with hundreds of aerial roots growing down toward the earth to become new trunks. Emerge into sunshine amid more guava trees, where for a time you can glimpse the mountains ahead above a waving sea of bamboo. Reenter the forest, and at about the 1-mile point cross a bridge over the stream, then promptly cross back over on a second bridge.

The trail enters a magical region—a very tall, very dense bamboo forest where the KLOK-KLOK sound of the stems knocking together in the wind makes weird and beautiful music and the rest of the world disappears. The illusion is

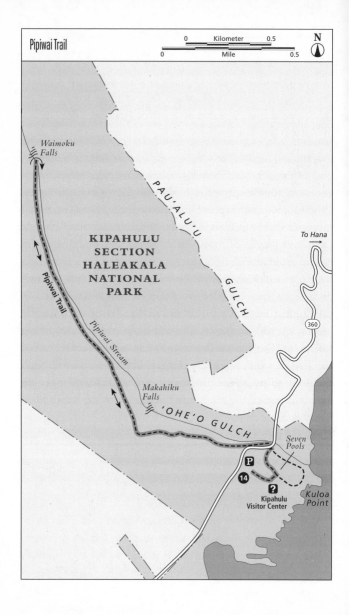

0       Kilometer       0.5

0           Mile           0.5

N

*Waimoku Falls*

PAU'ALU'U GULCH

**KIPAHULU SECTION HALEAKALA NATIONAL PARK**

*To Hana*

360

*Pipiwai Trail*

*Pipiwai Stream*

*Makahiku Falls*

'OHE'O GULCH

*Seven Pools*

P

14

?

*Kipahulu Visitor Center*

*Kuloa Point*

slightly disturbed by the recycled plastic faux-wood board-walk that has been installed to keep you off the muddy path and to prevent erosion caused by countless tourist feet.

When you finally emerge from the bamboo forest, round a corner, climb some big steps, rock hop a little stream, and enter a different kind of forest altogether. The canopy is made up of flamboyant African tulip trees, with gigantic red flowers and huge bird's-nest ferns clinging to their branches. These alternate with silvery *kukui* trees, whose nut shells pave the forest floor like cobblestones.

Cross another stream on slippery rocks, and in a few more yards find yourself at the edge of a pool beneath Waimoku Falls. It flows over the cliff 400 feet above in beautiful filmy patterns, with hundreds of tiny rivulets trickling from cracks in the rocks, nourishing rock gardens of delicate ferns. You're in a kind of lava amphitheater, surrounded by falling water and hanging gardens. This is a perfect spot to sit and have lunch or a snack, and you can splash in the pool and shower under the falls. Be aware, though, that rocks sometimes get washed over the cliff into the pool, so swim and shower at your own risk. Return the way you came.

## Miles and Directions

**0.0** Start at visitor center parking lot

**1.8** Waimoku Falls (N20 40.44' / W156 03.24')

**3.6** Arrive back at the trailhead

# 15  Hosmer Grove

Hosmer Grove may be the best place on Maui to see rare native Hawaiian birds with very little effort. In fact, you're likely to spot some interesting species even before you leave the parking lot. The hike is a cool, sometimes wet, ramble at almost 7,000 feet, through a forest of both introduced and native Hawaiian trees. At a clearing partway along the trail an interpretive panel helps you identify the birds that are likely to show up.

**Distance:** 0.6-mile loop
**Elevation gain:** About 100 feet
**Approximate hiking time:** 30 to 45 minutes
**Trail surface:** Worn lava
**Seasons:** Year-round
**Other trail users:** None
**Canine compatibility:** Dogs not permitted
**Fees and permits:** No permits are needed. A national park entrance fee is levied.
**Schedule:** Anytime

**Land status:** Haleakala National Park
**Maps:** *USGS Kilohana,* but none needed. The trail is short and well marked, and there is a map display at the trailhead. You can also find a map, as well as a trail guide, online at www.hear .org/usgs-brd-pierc-hfs/hosmer grove.htm.
**Trail contact:** Haleakala National Park headquarters; (808) 572-4400; www.nps.gov/hale

**Finding the trailhead:** From Kahului drive southeast on Highway 37 (the Haleakala Highway) for about 7 miles through the town of Pukalani. Just past town turn left (east) onto Highway 377, remaining on the Haleakala Highway. In another 6 miles you'll reach Highway 378, also known as Haleakala Crater Road, where you turn left (east) again to begin the slow, switchbacking ascent to the Hosmer Grove turnoff, which is on the left (east) about 10 miles up. If you find yourself at park headquarters (on the right, southwest) you've gone too far. Turn left and follow the road to the campground. Hosmer Grove has a free, first-come, first-served campground with water and toilets nearby. **Trailhead GPS:** N20 46.04' / W156 14.04'

## The Hike

The trail begins at a sign at the low end of the campground, where interpretive panels describe the history of the place and the fate of many of Hawaii's native species.

The grove is planted with trees from all over the world, including pines, spruces, cedars, and redwoods. It was a misguided attempt by forester Ralph Hosmer, in 1910, to slow the rate of deforestation occurring at an alarming rate in Hawai'i, and perhaps to establish a timber industry at the same time. Now, of course, some of these alien trees themselves pose a threat to the local ecosystem. Still, the variety of vegetation does attract a variety of birds, and there are still plenty of *ohia lehua* trees and other natives to appeal to *i'iwis*, *apapanes, amakihis,* and even Hawaiian owls.

Begin by crossing a little stream, then climb to an overlook where the park service has installed a panel to help you identify the birds. It's above an opening in the foliage of the canopy to give you a better view. Be patient and spend at least ten to fifteen minutes here, and you're bound to see something beautiful and rare.

Beyond the overlook is a junction where you keep left (north), heading uphill. The path to the right cuts straight back down to the campground. Climb through native scrubland, with fuzzy red *ohia* blossoms, short-leaved shrubs with pink and white berries called *pukiawe*, delicious plump *ohelo* berries, silvery *hinahina* geraniums, and the beautiful yellow-flowered pea called *mamane*. The trail tops out at a little bench where you can catch your breath and soak up the view before following the rest of the loop back down to the parking lot.

A wonderful little book that is easy to carry and shows all the birds you're likely to see in Hawai'i—and where to see them—is *Hawaii's Birds,* published by the Hawai'i Audubon Society in Honolulu.

# 16 Halemau'u Haleakala Overlook

Haleakala, the House of the Sun, was so named when Hina, mother of the demigod Maui, complained that the days were too short to allow her *tapa* cloth to dry. She would have to fold it up still damp and the designs would be smeared. Maui went to the mountain, lassoed a ray of the sun, and would not let it go until it promised to move more slowly across the sky so the days would last longer. Most people view the crater named Haleakala from its southeastern end, near the visitor center. This upside-down hike, descending to the rim at the northwestern end of Haleakala, allows for a mind-boggling view into the volcano. Winding through a region of classic Hawaiian native scrub vegetation, it is very different from the busier Sliding Sands Trail, which drops into the crater from the southwestern end. You really should try both.

**Distance:** 2.4 miles out and back

**Elevation loss:** 400 feet

**Approximate hiking time:** 1.5 to 2.5 hours

**Trail surface:** Worn lava

**Seasons:** Year-round, but expect more rain in winter (and on rare occasions snow)

**Other trail users:** None

**Canine compatibility:** Dogs not permitted

**Fees and permits:** No permits are required. A park entrance fee is levied.

**Schedule:** Anytime

**Land status:** Haleakala National Park

**Maps:** *USGS Kilohana; National Geographic–Trails Illustrated map of Haleakala National Park*

**Trail contact:** Haleakala National Park headquarters; (808) 572-4400; www.nps.gov/hale

**Finding the trailhead:** From Kahului drive southeast on Highway 37 (the Haleakala Highway) for about 7 miles through the town of

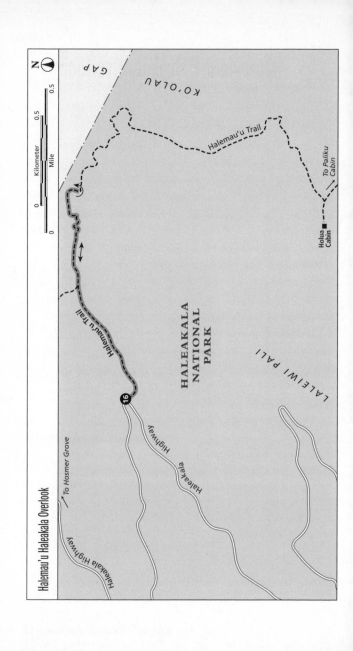

Halemau'u Haleakala Overlook

To Hosmer Grove

Haleakala Highway

Haleakala Highway

16

Halemau'u Trail

HALEAKALA
NATIONAL
PARK

LALEIWI PALI

Halemau'u Trail

To Paliku
Cabin

Holua
Cabin

KO'OLAU

GAP

N

0    Kilometer    0.5

0    Mile    0.5

Pukalani. Just past town turn left (east) onto Highway 377, staying on the Haleakala Highway. Travel another 6 miles to Highway 378, also known as Haleakala Crater Road (still called Haleakala Highway on the USGS topo), where you turn left (east) again to begin a slow, switchbacking ascent. Pass the park headquarters and continue for 3 miles more. Just past a sharp bend is the Halemau'u Trailhead, on the left (east). You'll find plenty of parking and pit toilets at the trailhead, but no water. **Trailhead GPS: N20 45.11' / W156 13.45'**

## The Hike

The Halemau'u Trailhead is a favorite hangout for *nene* geese, which relish the mist-fed grass that grows here, but they also practice looking pitifully hungry so tourists will toss them a few crumbs of more interesting treats. Please do not give in. They are just coming back from the brink of extinction and do not need junk food.

The trail begins a gentle descent through typical Hawaiian subalpine scrubland consisting of yellow-flowered *mamane* bushes, white-flowered, silvery-leaved *hinahina* geraniums, and *pukiawe* shrubs studded with tasteless (in flavor, not appearance) pink and white berries. The trail trends generally eastward toward Ko'olau Gap, where clouds swirl and tumble and pile up from below, and, if conditions are right, drift into the crater a wisp at a time.

The fence you might notice now and then runs around the entire perimeter of Haleakala, keeping out goats that would otherwise chew the native vegetation to stubble. In about 0.5 mile a trail climbing up from Hosmer Grove joins this one, and shortly thereafter the route makes a dogleg turn to the south and steepens. The braided, twisting *pahoehoe* flow that poured through the gap and down the mountainside looks as though it might have solidified only yesterday except for the tinge of green vegetation on its surface.

At 1.2 miles you round a corner and find yourself on the inside of Haleakala Crater, your turnaround point. The switchbacks below you head toward Holua Cabin, 2.6 rugged miles farther.

From the end of the route you can look westward to another break in the crater wall where the clouds creep—or sweep—in. This is Kaupo Gap. These openings in the crater wall keep the western end of the crater green while the eastern portion is a barren—but beautiful—cinder desert. The pathway that might be visible on the farthest red slope is the Sliding Sands Trail, heading up to the visitor center.

## Miles and Directions

**0.0** Halemau'u Trailhead

**0.5** Junction with the trail from Hosmer Grove (N20 45.21' / W156 17.21')

**1.2** Turnaround at viewpoint into Haleakala Crater (N20 45.22' / W156 12.57')

**2.4** Arrive back at the trailhead

# 17  Red Hill Summit Overlook

Stand on the highest point on the island of Maui—Pu'u Ula'ula or Red Hill at more than 10,000 feet—where (if the weather is clear) the views will knock your socks off! You can look right down into the colorful crater of Haleakala volcano, as well as out to sea to several other Hawaiian Islands. It's going to be much colder than you expect at this elevation. Dress appropriately.

**Distance:** 0.2 mile out ad back
**Elevation gain:** 50 feet
**Approximate hiking time:** 15 to 20 minutes
**Trail surface:** Asphalt
**Seasons:** Year-round. Rain is more likely in winter. Views are better earlier in the day as clouds gather in the afternoon.
**Other trail users:** None
**Canine compatibility:** Dogs not permitted
**Fees and permits:** No permits required; park entrance fee

**Schedule entry:** Sunrise to sunset
**Land status:** Haleakala National Park
**Maps:** USGS quad Kilohana; no map needed, though the National Geographic–Trails Illustrated map of Haleakala National Park will help you identify some of the features you can see from the summit
**Trail contact:** Haleakala National Park headquarters; (808) 572-4400; www.nps.gov/hale

**Finding the trailhead:** From Kahului drive southeast on the Haleakala Highway (Highway 37) for about 7 miles, through the town of Pukalani. Just past town turn left (east) onto Highway 377, remaining on the Haleakala Highway. Travel another 6 miles to Highway 378 (Haleakala Crater Road; still called Haleakala Highway on the USGS topo), where you turn left (east) again to begin the slow, switchbacking ascent to the park entrance. Park headquarters is on your right (west), roughly 11 miles. You can pay your entrance fee

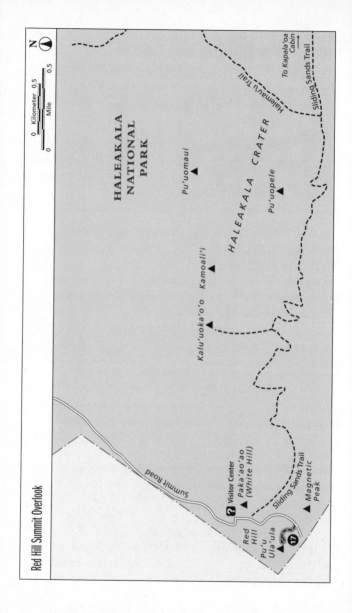

Red Hill Summit Overlook

here. The road continues steeply upward, with sharp switchbacking turns, for 11 more miles to the visitor center. Drive past the visitor center parking lot and turn right into the very first drive, which is the Red Hill parking lot. You'll find water and toilets here, but no food and no gas. **Trailhead GPS:** N20 42.47' / W156 15.04'

## The Hike

You'll know you're at the highest point on Maui as soon as you step out of your car, especially if you're not used to high elevations. The air is thinner and cooler at 10,000 feet.

A set of stairs leads up to an enclosed shelter with a 360-degree view into the wild, alien landscape of Haleakala Crater. You'll appreciate the shelter if you get there early enough in the day for the best views. It's very cold in the mornings. You can also get a good look at Science City, an assemblage of futuristic observatories and other buildings. The path follows the rim of the hill above the parking lot and offers views of West Maui, the other volcano that, along with Haleakala, makes up the island of Maui. You should also be able to see the Big Island of Hawai'i, Lanai, Moloka'i, and Kaho'olawe, until recently used as a bombing practice range by the U.S. military.

In the center of the parking lot you'll find a little garden where the wonderful spiky silver rosettes of silverswords grow. These striking plants live nowhere else in the world.

There's usually a ranger around to answer questions, and interpretive signs reminding you that the barren-seeming lava underfoot shelters many fragile organisms that may be destroyed if you stray from the trail.

# 18  Into Haleakala Crater

Sliding Sands (*Keonehe'ehe'e* in Hawaiian) is the easiest trail into and out of Haleakala Crater, with fabulous views all the way. This hike is at the more strenuous end of "easy," but you can turn around whenever you like and it's a great opportunity to sample the eerie landscape inside a dormant volcanic crater and to see some of Maui's beautiful and endangered flowers, silverswords.

**Distance:** 4 miles out and back
**Elevation loss:** 1,200 feet
**Approximate hiking time:** 2 to 4 hours
**Trail surface:** Mostly packed sand and cinders
**Seasons:** Year-round, but it does occasionally snow in winter
**Other trail users:** Equestrians
**Canine compatibility:** Dogs not permitted
**Fees and permits:** No permit is needed for a day hike. A fee to enter the park is levied.
**Schedule:** Sunrise to sunset
**Land status:** Haleakala National Park
**Maps:** *USGS Kilohana; National Geographic–Trails Illustrated Haleakala National Park* map

**Trail contact:** Haleakala National Park headquarters; (808) 572-4400; www.nps.gov/hale
**Special considerations:** Be prepared for rapid and extreme weather changes on the mountain. Cold wind and rain can suddenly blow in through gaps in the crater wall, and there is very little shelter. Carry rain gear. On the other hand, tropical sun reflecting off black rock can be scorching, and there is no potable water on this hike. Carry lots of water and sunscreen. Guided horseback tours use this trail regularly. Remember that horses always have right of way, so please stop, step to the side, and stand quietly until they have passed.

**Finding the trailhead:** From Kahului drive southeast on Highway 37 (the Haleakala Highway) for about 7 miles, through the town of

Pukalani. Just past town turn left (east) onto Highway 377, staying on the Haleakala Highway. Travel for another 6 miles to Highway 378 (Haleakala Crater Road; still called Haleakala Highway on the USGS topo), and turn left (east) again to begin the slow, switchbacking ascent. Pass park headquarters, continuing up the road to the visitor center and parking lot on the rim of the crater. You'll find water and toilets here, but no food and no gas. **Trailhead GPS:** N20 42.47' / W156 15.04'

## The Hike

A sign at the visitor center points to the trailhead. Pass the hitching rail where the horses are tied in the parking lot, walk left for a few paces along the summit road, then swing left (east) again toward the crater rim. A good interpretive panel shows you what the mountain looked like at its height, and reminds you that this volcano is only dormant, not extinct.

Now you plunge into a different world. The excellent, well-graded trail, with broad switchbacks, allows you to appreciate the stupendous views without having to watch your feet. Usually you can see the clouds crowding into the Kaupo Gap on the right (southeast) and the Ko'olau Gap on the left (northeast), while most of the time the crater floor remains clear. A little less than 2 miles down the trail you'll see your first silverswords. They form rounded clumps of silvery, swordlike leaves that bide their time for anywhere from seven to thirty years, storing up energy for the day when each thrusts a flowering stalk as high as 9 feet, covered with big, purple, daisylike flowers. They die after flowering. Silverswords are extremely rare and grow nowhere else in the world but here.

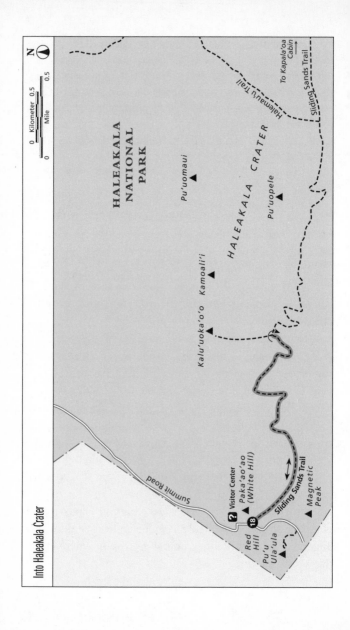

Into Haleakala Crater

HALEAKALA
NATIONAL
PARK

HALEAKALA CRATER

Pu'uomaui

Kalu'uoka'o'o

Kamoali'i

Pu'uopele

To Kapala'oa
Cabin

Sliding Sands Trail

Halemau'u Trail

Summit Road

Visitor Center

Paka'ao'ao (White Hill)

18

Red Hill

Pu'u Ula'ula

Sliding Sands Trail

Magnetic Peak

N

0    Kilometer    0.5
0         Mile         0.5

At 2 miles meet the cutoff trail to Kalu'uoka'o'o cone, your turnaround point. Return as you came.

## Miles and Directions

**0.0**  Trailhead

**2.0**  Trail to Kalu'uoka'o'o crater; turnaround point (N20 42.41' / W156 14.00')

**4.0**  Arrive back at the trailhead

**Option:** You can continue for another 1.2 miles round-trip down to the rim of Kalu'uoka'o'o, a beautiful, multicolored crater, for an even more intimate experience inside a volcano. Just remember that it's a lot slower and more strenuous climbing uphill. Make sure you have plenty of water, time, and energy for the long haul back up to almost 10,000 feet.

# 19 Ma'alaea Beach Walk

This is a stroll along a smooth, sandy beach. As part of the Kealia Pond National Wildlife Refuge, these few miles of seashore between noisy, hectic Kihei to the south and busy Ma'alaea Village to the north are much less crowded than most of the island's beaches. Birders can watch for some of the native and migratory bird species that inhabit the adjoining wetland.

**Distance:** 4 miles out and back
**Elevation change:** None
**Approximate hiking time:** 2 hours (or less)
**Trail surface:** Sand
**Other trail users:** None
**Canine compatibility:** Leashed dogs permitted
**Fees and permits:** None

**Schedule:** Sunrise to sunset
**Land Status:** Kealia Pond National Wildlife Refuge
**Map:** *USGS quad Maalaea,* but none needed
**Trail contact:** Kealia Pond National Wildlife Refuge; (808) 875-1582

**Finding the trailhead:** From the Kahului Airport turn right (north) on Highway 36, left (west) on Kamehameha Avenue, then left again (south) on Pu'unene Avenue. Pu'unene Avenue turns into Mokulele Highway (Highway 311), and continues south. When you reach Kihei Road (Highway 31) turn right (northwest), and go past a series of condos on the left (*makai/*toward the ocean). Where the condos end look for a place to park on the left side of the highway by the beach. Mile marker 3 is a good place to start. A sign on the other side of the street marks the Kealia Pond National Wildlife Refuge. **Trailhead GPS:** N20 47.16' / W156 28.14'

# The Hike

Go through a gap in the rickety fence and head west along the shore. You are never far from the highway, but the roar of the surf on one side and *kiawe* trees on the other allow you to forget about the road most of the time. You are in the curve of the isthmus of the island, with the West Maui mountains in front of you and Haleakala behind. There aren't many shells to admire on this beach but there are hunks of coral and tube worm casts washed up on the sand. Little crabs and seabirds scuttle along the shore and, especially when the tide is out, there are worn pockets in the polished lava where you can watch tiny sea creatures cling and crawl. Patches of bright green beach morning glories with purple flowers sprawl over the sand in places. You might also be able to spot Kaho'olawe, the devastated island used as a practice bombing range by the U.S. military from the 1940s to the 1990s.

In about 1 mile you'll reach a new boardwalk on the highway side of the beach, raised a bit so you can look over the highway to the right (northeast) to the wetlands section of the Kealia Pond National Wildlife Refuge. The boardwalk is less than 0.5-mile long, but crosses a portion of Kealia Pond, where you might spot some native wading birds. You can also remain on (or return to) the beach and continue walking for about another 0.5 mile, until you draw close enough to the next cluster of condos to end the undeveloped section of the shore. Return the way you came.

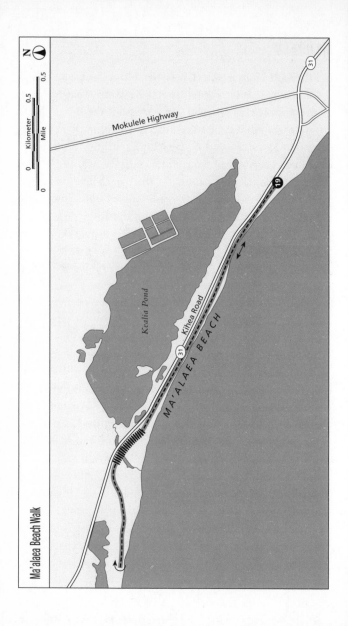

# Miles and Directions

**0.0** Begin on the beach at mile marker 3

**1.3** Beginning of boardwalk (N20 47.43' / W156 29.07')

**2.0** Turnaround point (N20 27.48' / W156 29.48')

**4.0** Arrive back at the trailhead

# 20  Olowalu Petroglyphs

These are some of the most accessible petroglyphs on Maui (not counting those on hotel grounds, some of which are reproductions). The petroglyphs are incised geometric designs and stylized human figures whose meanings are unknown. They are in fairly good condition, though there has been some vandalism. The Hike is short and mostly level, but can be hot and is best done early or on an overcast day.

**Distance:** 1.2 miles out and back
**Elevation gain:** 40 feet
**Approximate hiking time:** 40 minutes to 1 hour
**Trail surface:** Dirt road
**Seasons:** Year-round, but hot in summer
**Other trail users:** Cyclists; occasional cars
**Canine compatibility:** Dogs permitted
**Fees and permits:** None
**Schedule:** Anytime
**Land status:** Private
**Map:** *USGS Olowalu*
**Trail contact:** None

**Finding the trailhead:** From the Kahului Airport take Highway 380 (the Kuihelani Highway) south to Highway 30 (the Honoapi'ilani Highway). Turn left (south) and continue about 12 miles to the Olowalu Store and Chez Paul Restaurant. You won't miss them: There isn't much else there. Pull around in back of the store and park by a water tank at a road that runs *mauka* (toward the mountain), perpendicular to the highway. You'll see an open gate and a sign that says OLOWALU PETROGLYPHS. Please stay on the road and do not block the gate since this is private land. **Trailhead GPS:** N20 48.44' / W156 37.21'

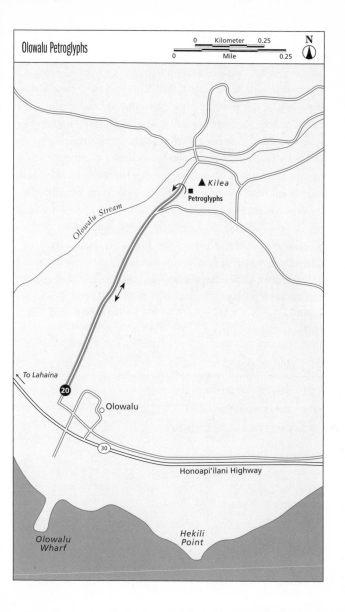

# The Hike

Follow the dirt road *mauka* (toward the mountain) through weedy wasteland and cane fields. You will see a paved road swing off to your right (east), but stay on the main (dirt) road, ignoring any side trips. A small volcanic cone to the right (northeast), at the mouth of a valley, marks the spot.

Cross over an irrigation ditch and look for some iron railings on the hillside on your right, behind a tin shack. These lead up to what used to be a viewing platform. Scramble up the slope over chunks of broken concrete to a level spot and look to the left (north) to see the petroglyphs. The designs are similar to those all over the Hawaiian Islands, so they surely have some religious significance, but their meaning has been lost. They are not in the best condition, but very much worth seeing. While you're in the area you can enjoy other amenities: Olowalu has good snorkeling and Chez Paul is a fine restaurant.

## Miles and Directions

- **0.0** Start
- **0.6** Petroglyphs (N20 49.07' / W156 37.07')
- **1.2** Arrive back at the trailhead

# About the Author

Suzanne Swedo, director of W.I.L.D. (natural history adventures around the world), has backpacked the mountains of every continent. She has led groups into the wilderness for more than twenty-five years and teaches wilderness survival and natural sciences for individuals, schools, universities, museums, and organizations such as the Yosemite Association and the Sierra Club. She is author of *Best Easy Day Hikes Yosemite National Park, Hiking Yosemite, Hiking California's Golden Trout Wilderness,* and *Adventure Travel Tips,* all FalconGuides. She lectures and consults about backpacking, botany, and survival on radio and television, as well as in print. While she lives in Los Angeles, California, she has been leading hiking groups in Hawai'i for more than twenty-five years.

# WHAT'S SO SPECIAL ABOUT UNSPOILED, NATURAL PLACES?

Beauty   Solitude   Wildness   Freedom   Quiet   Adventure
Serenity   Inspiration   Wonder   Excitement
Relaxation                    Challenge

There's a lot to love about our treasured public lands, and the reasons are different for each of us. Whatever your reasons are, the national **Leave No Trace** education program will help you discover special outdoor places, enjoy them, and preserve them—today and for those who follow.  By practicing and passing along these simple principles, you can help protect the special places you love from being loved to death.

## THE PRINCIPLES OF **LEAVE NO TRACE**

- Plan ahead and prepare
- Travel and camp on durable surfaces
- Dispose of waste properly
- Leave what you find
- Minimize campfire impacts
- Respect wildlife
- Be considerate of other visitors

## AMERICAN HIKING SOCIETY

Because you

hike.

We're with you
every step of the way

American Hiking Society gives voice to the more than 75 million Americans who hike and is the only national organization that promotes and protects foot trails, the natural areas that surround them, and the hiking experience. Our work is inspiring and challenging, and is built on three pillars:

### Volunteerism and Stewardship

We organize and coordinate nationally recognized programs—including Volunteer Vacations, National Trails Day ®, and the National Trails Fund— that help keep our trails open, safe, and enjoyable.

### Policy and Advocacy

We work with Congress and federal agencies to ensure funding for trails, the preservation of natural areas, and the protection of the hiking experience.

### Outreach and Education

We expand and support the national constituency of hikers through outreach and education as well as partnerships with other recreation and conservation organizations.

**Join us in our efforts. Become an American Hiking Society member today!**

American
Hiking
Society

1422 Fenwick Lane · Silver Spring, MD 20910 · (800) 972-8608
www.AmericanHiking.org · info@AmericanHiking.org